Living Lagom:

A Swedish Guide to a Balanced Life

Maya Thoresen

© 2018

© Copyright 2018 by Maya Thoresen - All rights reserved.

The following eBook is reproduced below with the goal of providing information that is as accurate and as reliable as possible. Regardless, purchasing this eBook can be seen as consent to the fact that both the publisher and the author of this book are in no way experts on the topics discussed within, and that any recommendations or suggestions made herein are for entertainment purposes only. Professionals should be consulted as needed before undertaking any of the action endorsed herein.

This declaration is deemed fair and valid by both the American Bar Association and the Committee of Publishers Association and is legally binding throughout the United States.moreover , the transmission, duplication or reproduction of any of the following work, including precise information, will be considered an illegal act, irrespective whether it is done electronically or in print. The legality extends to creating a secondary or tertiary copy of the work or a recorded copy and is only allowed with the express written consent of the Publisher. All additional rights are reserved.

The information in the following pages is broadly considered to be a truthful and accurate account of facts, and as such any inattention, use or misuse of the information in question by the reader will render any resulting actions solely under their purview. There are no scenarios in which the publisher or the original author of this work can be in any fashion deemed liable for any hardship or damages that may befall them after undertaking information described herein.

Additionally, the information found on the following pages is intended for informational purposes only and should thus be considered universal. As befitting its nature, the information presented is without assurance regarding its continued validity or interim quality. Trademarks that are mentioned are done without written consent and can in no way be considered an endorsement from the trademark holder.

ISBN 978-1-953714-22-0

Contents

WHAT IS LAGOM?...7

LAGOM IN SWEDEN AND AROUND THE WORLD........11

LAGOM, HAPPINESS AND HYGIENE......................15

LAGOM IN PERSONAL LIFE, FAMILY, AND RELATIONSHIPS
....21

LAGOM AT HOME..27

    BEDROOM...28
    LIVING ROOM...29
    KITCHEN AND DINING ROOM............................29
    BATHROOM..30

LAGOM HEALTH AND WELLBEING.........................37

LAGOM IN THE KITCHEN..43

    BREAKFAST...44
    SANDWICHES..46
    LUNCH AND DINNER...48
    JUNK FOOD...55
    SNACKS...58

LAGOM AS A WAY OF SAVING THE PLANET..........63
LAGOM CLOTHING..................................69
LAGOM AND PARENTING............................73
LAGOM HOBBIES....................................77
PETS AND LAGOM..................................81
SPORTS AND LAGOM...............................85
LAGOM WHILE TRAVELING.........................89
LAGOM THROUGHOUT THE SEASONS................93

    SPRING..94
    SUMMER...95
    FALL..96
    WINTER...97

21-DAY LAGOM CHALLENGE.........................99
CONCLUSION......................................106

CHAPTER 1: WHAT IS LAGOM?

Lagom (pronounced [làːgɔm]) is a Swedish word used to describe the perfect state when something is neither too much, nor too little, it is just enough to make you satisfied. It can be used when talking about anything from the weather Know the amount of milk you pour in your coffee. If the question starts with "how much?" the typical answer in Sweden is "lagom." There are a few words that can be used to relate to lagom; for example, "enough," "moderate," and "balanced." Each of these concepts contributes to the overall meaning of lagom. The true meaning of lagom, however, is a way of expressing when something is just enough.

Etymologically, the term "lagom" is a combination of the two words "lag" and "om." Centuries ago, there was a lack of food, resulting in only one plate of food per household, which had to be enough to go around the table. No one at the table could take too much food. In Swedish "lag" means "team," or "table," and "om" means "around." "Lagom", therefore, implies around the table. This explanation makes sense, although nowadays, historians and etymologists believe that this may be a myth constructed more recently.

Lagom is used to describe a feeling of satisfaction or when something is enough. We all have a different perception of when we are content and satisfied, which makes the definition a bit difficult to pin down, but this is the essence of lagom. There is no general description or measurement of how much lagom is, which makes it quite a complicated concept. There are as many definitions for lagom as there are Swedish people. How much each one considers to be satisfying is a matter of taste, and it can be difficult even for the Swedish to understand what someone else considers to be lagom. Of course, it is a constant source of discussion and friendly debate amongst friends, families, and couples when one of them wants lagom and gets either too much or too little. This usually happens when one person neglects to ask the other how much he or she considers to be lagom. It is easy to give someone else what we ourselves believe to be the right amount. Of course, frequent misunderstandings are expected, especially when new acquaintances are still determining each other's definition and taste. However, the misunderstandings are neither serious nor the source of any huge conflict at all amongst the Swedish people, as they are considered a part of everyday life. For most individuals, there lies a silent agreement to disagree on the definition and accept that everyone thinks differently.

If there is no real definition of lagom, then why use it? To those who are not Swedish, the definition is strange and complicated, and it can be debated whether anything is truly lagom. Distinguishing lagom is like comparing food that is too hot or not hot enough, too sweet or not sweet enough, and so on. Despite these constant complaints, the Swedish people are quite content with everything when asked to seriously consider the situation. Perhaps these minor complaints are a way for the Swedish people to connect to each other and start a conversation. They might be onto by something; accepting things as never quite lagom is being lagom in itself. From this aspect, the concept is not about a useless word, but instead is about a useful and satisfying concept that makes the Swedish people happy.
The question still remains: Why is lagom something to strive for if we are not able to agree on what lagom is?

It is complicated to apply logic and reason when lagom cannot have a proper, quantifiable definition. There is one more aspect of lagom, which we have not talked about yet. If we dropped the point of defining lagom, then the whole point is that there is no definition. Perhaps the meaning of lagom is to figure out what it is for you and live accordingly without being so concerned with other people's thinking.
Let's examine this further. In Sweden, the general mentality is "each to his own"In other words, don't interfere in other people's lives when they have not asked for it, and let them express their opinions and live life on their terms. Lagom is something that needs to be figured out independently and then applied to life. There is no right or wrong definition of lagom; it is a grey zone that is defined independently and expressed differently by each person. The aspect of lagom and its definition is beautiful because it holds space for interpretation for each person.

Lagom cannot be defined as one single, universal statement, but an independent one that each individual has to define on their own. As your life and your perspective changes, so can your definition of lagom. Lagom is always in tune with you.

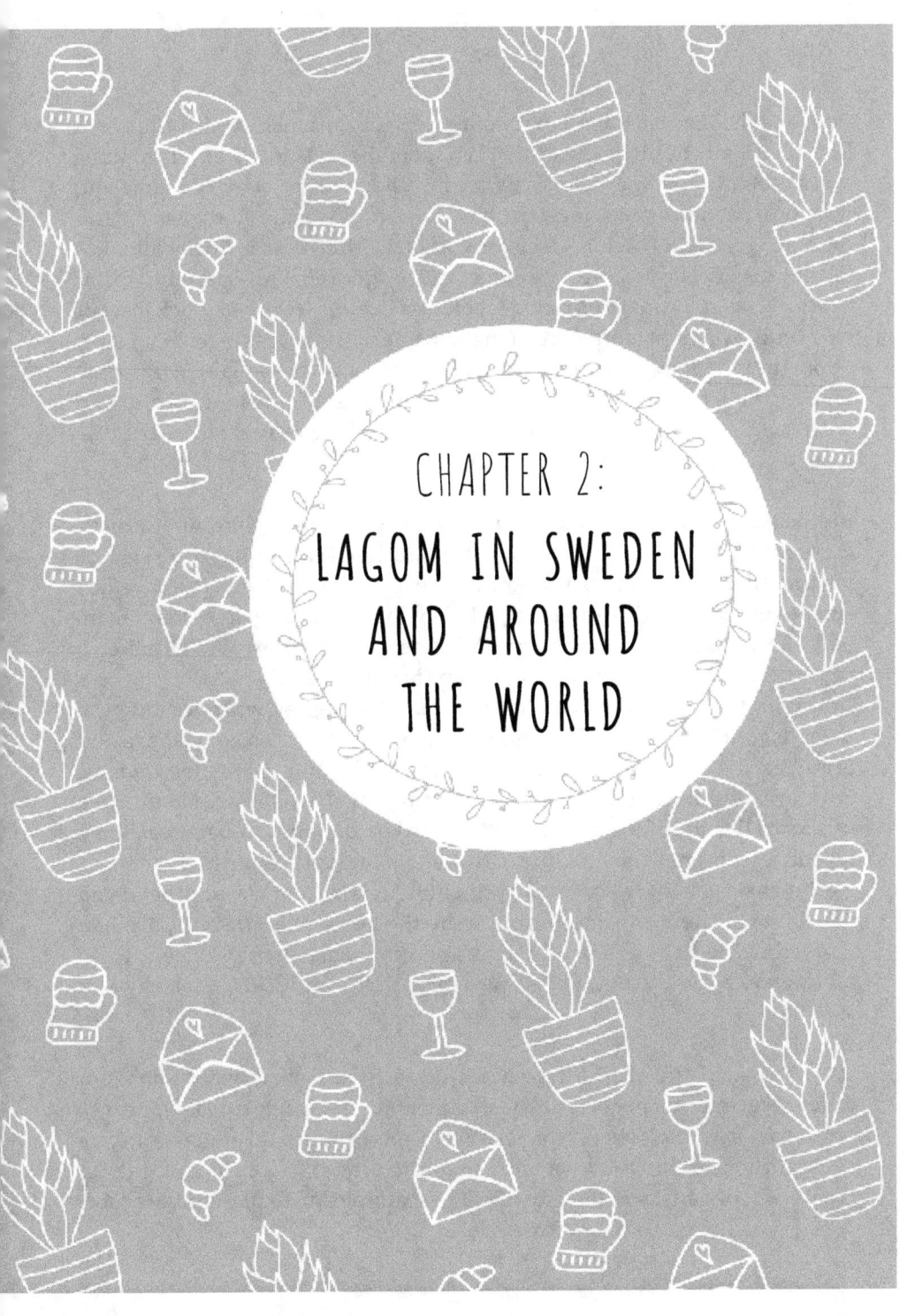

CHAPTER 2:
LAGOM IN SWEDEN AND AROUND THE WORLD

CHAPTER 2: LAGOM IN SWEDEN AND AROUND THE WORLD

In this chapter, you'll learn how the Swedish people view lagom, which is different from how the rest of the world may see it.

The Swedish have a somewhat complicated relationship with the word lagom and all that it stands for. The lagom lifestyle is a way of thinking and acting that is deeply internalized in the Swedish way of being, and they don't tend to consciously think about it. It is a life that goes on and on in a nice little track of decisions, and the fact that it does so makes lagom go by unnoticed, perhaps even ignored. Alternately, other Swedies are sick and tired being labeled as lagom. They feel stuck in a rut and tend to feel ashamed at being considered moderate, seizing every opportunity trying to break free. It is not easy to explain why some Swedes have this feeling. Perhaps they don't want to be labeled and and wish to escape from the term, while others just ignore or live with the label that has been imposed on them.

Besides the anti-lagom population, Swedish people in general are more careful to keep their lives lagom-style, rather than living too large or putting themselves in a situation where they are noticed. The Swedish can be regarded as content being labeled "lagom" as they live their lagom lives. Perhaps some of them have become more comfortable with being lagom as the rest of the world picks up this lifestyle.

In the previous chapter, you learned about struggles with defining the term "lagom." This difficulty comes from other countries being more and more fascinated with the phenomenon and adopting it for their own. It is interesting how a rather small country like Sweden can influence others to live a different kind of life in order to maintain balance. Some Swedish state that they maintain the lagom lifestyle because they find it as the easiest way to live a sustainable, healthy, happy, and balanced life. Some of them consider lagom to be the perfect interstitial path in a divided world full of contradictions and non-consequent advice. Lagom allows you to enjoy all the little pleasures in life and still be healthy and satisfied.

To the rest of the world, lagom seems to be a clever way to make a difference and turn certain events around in order to make things better. In a world where we face huge environmental issues and are constantly searching for ways to save the planet, lagom might, in fact create a more sustainable lifestyle. For example, instead of buying food that goes uneaten, people can buy only the necessary amount. This goes for clothes and everything else as well; buy only what you need and what you will use. To the rest of the world, lagom might be a way to describe the "quality over quantity" mindset. This can save you time and money in the long run. This is also applicable to the "work as well as home" balance many of us struggle to find. Instead of working too much and spending little time with our children, strive to do everything lagom-style to make time for both the business and pleasure aspects of ife without facing a burnout. These are some of the reasons why the world is fascinated and inspired by Sweden and lagom.

While some of the Swedish people are sick and tired of being caught in this grey scale of life where everything is lagom, in moderation, and just enough to satisfy them, people in other parts of the world are turning their eyes to Sweden as a leading example of a sustainable, healthy, and happy lifestyle.

Chapter 3: Lagom, Happiness and Hygiene

CHAPTER 3: LAGOM, HAPPINESS AND HYGIENE

- We have already touched on how lagom can be connected to happiness and how it can lead to a more harmonious life. In this chapter, we will dig deeper to discover more about this idea. In this book, when we raise the subject of lagom and its connection to happiness, keep in mind that we don't talk about happiness about an event or situation, but instead, we are referring to a subtle and calm feeling of joy. This type of feeling does overwhelm you if you aren't used to it, but rises from a place of satisfaction. You might also think of it as contentment.

Although some groups of the Swedish population are trying to break free from being labeled "lagom," Sweden has paved the way for a new method of achieving balance and also more happiness. Settling for lagom when you could be striving for more is not a bad idea; in fact, the Swedes are on to something. By settling for lagom, they don't take on more responsibilities than they are able to, and in doing so, they apply a sense of self-preservation and self-care. When settling occurs in your job and your life, there is no urgency to strive for more for yourself or for your family. Use the time to do things you enjoy that create happiness. Working constantly is not healthy for you, your mind, or your family, as your energy is depleted by work. Applying moderation in your life will create happiness and can increase the amount of contentment already present in your life.

To accomplish lagom, take a look at your life and analyze what is important to you. Take a look at your habits and consider how you can improve them. What's better way to use some extra time than to create a lifestyle that makes you happy? What makes us happy is specific to the individual, but whatever you like to do, using lagom in your life will make some time for your favorite things. It is important to remember that time is not the only connection between lagom and happiness -- it is contentment. Considering things to be "just good enough" rather than striving for perfection can save plenty of irritations and help you to a stress-free life. This process can take time, though. The first efforts of transitioning into a lagom mindset can be frustrating, as things can begin to pile up and not be completed. It is like quitting smoking or caffeine. It is frustrating at first, and you might have to abstain from certain things, but after a while, happiness will come easier to you than before.

When talking about lagom and finding happiness, there is another phenomenon worth mentioning. In Denmark, they have a concept called hygge [pronounced hoo-ga]. Hygge can be described as a warm, cozy, and comfortable atmosphere where you take the time to enjoy the good things in life with the people you love. Hygge is an activity, or a state of being, whereas lagom is a view on life and a way of living. Despite the differences, there is a connection to be found between hygge and lagom. They are both derived from a longing for slowing down and keeping things simple. Lagom is all about balance and moderation, and when experiencing hygge, you are spending your time in a moderate way. It is an easy-going atmosphere where nothing is too much or too little, but just lagom. Therefore, hygge is a lagom state of being, despite the lack of connection overall. While lagom and hygge are different connections to living and feeling, they are similar in cause and consequence. Apply lagom to your life to achieve balance and to find more time for the things you love to do. This extra time saved can be spent with family, friends, other loved ones, and hobbies in a cozy atmosphere called hygge. It all works out as a circle of being cozy and happy in your home as energy and money should not be wasted to enjoy life. In other words, hygge is lagom completely.

Like lagom, what makes something "hygge" is a matter of taste. To some people, it might be meeting some friends over dinner, catching up after work in a nice coffee shop, or a movie night with your family. The point of hygge is to be calm and cozy- to pass the time in such a way that you will be energized instead of burning negative energy constantly. Filling up your positive energy like this will result in a balanced, happy, and content life. Furthermore, enjoying the little things in life can improve your ability to handle stress like a mediocre job, a mean colleague at work, or any of the small, annoying things that occur in everyday life. Lagom and hygge are very similar concepts, although they also have some differences. It's important to understand both of these concepts separately when you're trying to live a lagom lifestyle so you can more easily determine which elements to incorporate into your way of living. Read through the lists below to help you get a better idea of what to expect from both hygge and lagom. This way, you'll know when you're practicing a habit that falls into one more than the other, and you'll be better able to choose the right methods of improving your lifestyle regardless of which category they may fall into.

ELEMENTS OF HYGGE:

- Hygge is designed to help you feel cozy. At its core, this concept is all about comfort and coziness in every aspect of your life. The warmer, the better!

- Hygge could include curling up and being comfortable in your favorite clothes, with your favorite blanket, and surrounded by soft lighting while you enjoy a hobby that helps you relax.

- Hygge focuses a lot on textures and relies on soft fabrics to help create the sense of coziness required for living this lifestyle.

- Colors associated with hygge include neutral and earthy tones such as cream, beige, tan, gray, dark brown, gold, and silver.

- There's more to hygge than just physical comfort; it is also about being comfortable around your friends and family. This concept involves relaxation and the kind of happiness you feel when you're with the people you love.

ELEMENTS OF LAGOM:

- Lagom is about enjoying the quality of your life instead of feeling like you have to increase the quantity of the things you own. Minimalism is where lagom really shines. The more minimalistic you are, the better you'll be at bringing this concept into your home and life.

- One of the key points of lagom is making sure you live as sustainably as possible to reduce your carbon footprint. Your relationship with the environment is crucial to ensuring you have a great lagom experience.

- Textures aren't as important in lagom, but it is a good idea to introduce curves and gentle, flowing lines into your interior spaces rather than sticking with sharp, hard lines throughout your home to inspire an organic sense of peace of mind.

- When possible, choose handcrafted items as well as foods that are made from healthy, organic ingredients for your lagom lifestyle.

- Colors associated with lagom include neutral tones such as tan, off-white, and soft gray, as well as slot of starkly contrasting tones found in minimalist decor, such as black and white.

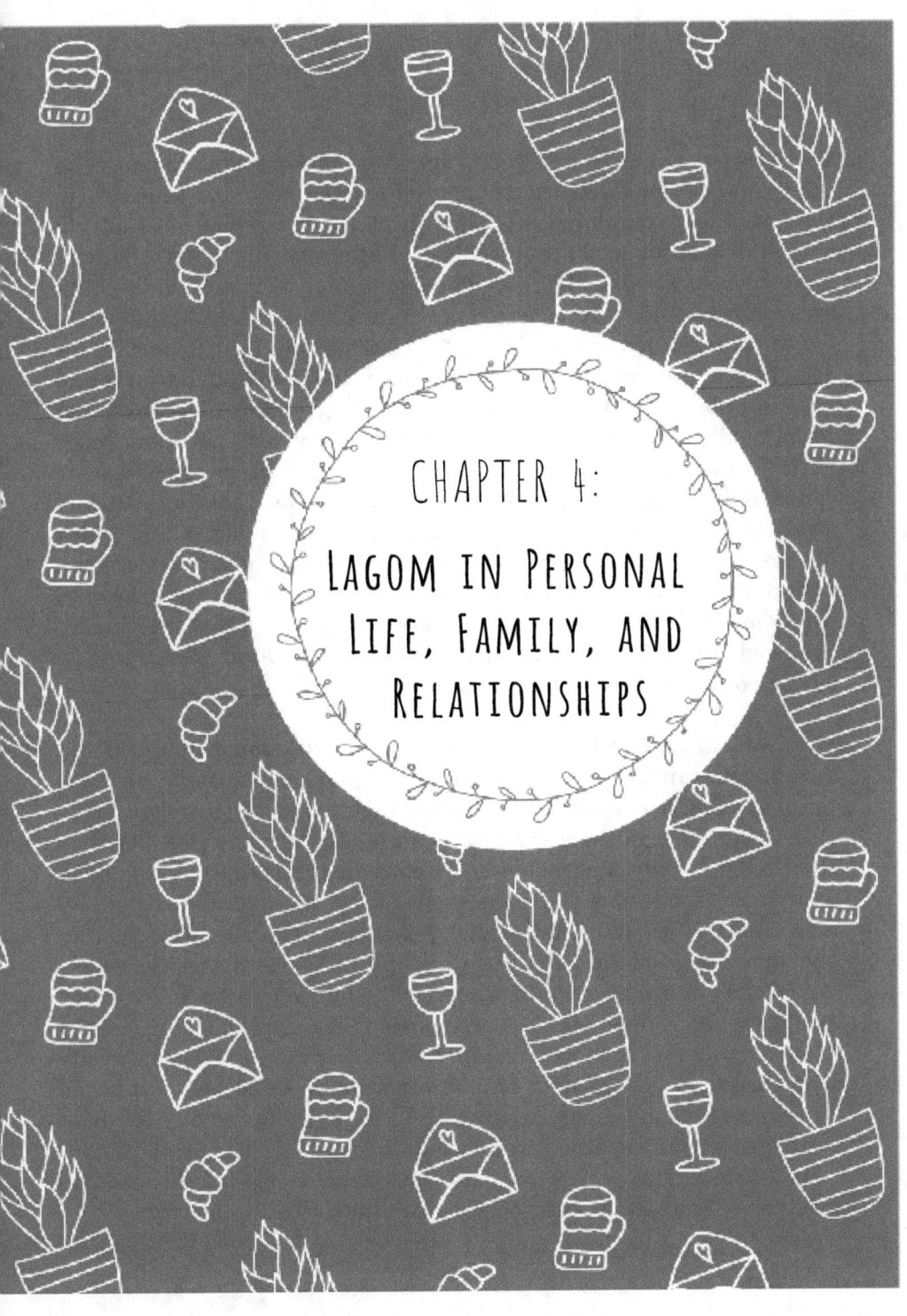

Chapter 4:
Lagom in Personal Life, Family, and Relationships

CHAPTER 4: LAGOM IN PERSONAL LIFE, FAMILY, AND RELATIONSHIPS

Now let's talk about how to apply lagom to your personal life, your time with family, friends, and others. Plus, you will learn how to set aside time and energy to enjoy special interests and hobbies.

We are encouraged from a young age to be social; spending time with others and working well in a group is a characteristic that is rewarded in today's society. Communication has always been stressed in society; in fact, guidelines for good people skills can be found in the New Testament. In Peter 4:8-9, we can find the following: "Above all, maintain constant love for one another, for love covers a multitude of sins. Be hospitable to one another without complaining". Social skills have been important for ages, but they are even Far more important today in both business and personal life. With the influence of technology, online marketing, and social media , it is even more important to stay social in order to be noticed and successful in your career. During spare time, staying connected to social media may seem relaxing but psychologically it isn't ideal for resting, as it keeps the mind alert. For some reason, being introverted and enjoying time alone and offline is almost considered an undesirable trait, and there are even courses to teach us how to overcome this behavior and become more social. It is a challenge to stay balanced and disconnect once in a while when the world is encouraging us to be online and connected constantly.

The Swedish, however, have a reputation of being somewhat cold and distant to strangers and to each other despite the want and need for social skills in their society. The truth is that the Swedish are not really anti-social. Most of them are just as social as everyone else, but they inherited the mindset of leaving each to his own. This concept, combined with their lagom lifestyle, gives them an air of solitude-seeking and loneliness in their life. The Swedish behavior is actually quite healthy and something for the rest of us to adopt. In Western society, we are forced to be social at work, in school, and wherever we spend our time during the day. Sometimes, the expectations are extremely high; we are expected to spend time with family, talk to coworkers and clients, study with classmates or teachers, and be cordial with colleagues and peers. This is stressful and can be exhausting. In the evening and on days off, it is still expected from others and society to be social when all our bodies need is sleep and rest. Filling up days with things to do leads to exhaustion and lost interest in passions. When transitioning to the lagom lifestyle, you might get frustrated and even hate doing things you usually enjoy with others just because you have been forced into everything and forced away from yourself. Therefore, it is important to keep in touch with yourself and your own interests in order to enjoy all of these social events that are quite nice when you find the perfect balance in socialization.

In Sweden, when people sit alone on the bus, or avoid talking to each other while waiting in line at the supermarket, they are creating a balance between social commitments and encouraging some recovery time. It is true that the Swedish are keener on minding their own business than many others, and this contributes to their lagom lifestyle. They could chat with the person next to them, but they don't, because they value personal space and privacy. In these situations, lagom does not mean staying at the house, locking yourself inside, and having scheduled time alone, because that does not work either. Instead, lagom is about being quiet while riding the bus or standing in line. It is not forced downtime alone, but rather a good compromise to recharge and have more energy once you get home to your family. By applying lagom this way, the Swedish have cracked the code of balance between being social and being alone. Instead of bending over backwards trying to keep up with all the social events and commitments, the Swedish people take care of their alone time. They spend time alone, either by themselves or with their family, allowing themselves time to recover and recharge from the social pressures of the world.

CHAPTER 4: LAGOM IN PERSONAL LIFE, FAMILY, AND RELATIONSHIPS

Once you take the time to rearrange your busy schedule and recharge properly, it is possible that you will want to take up a hobby. Hobbies are often the first to get eliminated as we become busy with work and family, despite their numerous health benefits. As discussed earlier, applying lagom leads to an increased amount of free time that you can use to recharge. Recharging energy levels can bring love and joy to previously enjoyed hobbies. The love and joy you find in a hobby can also generate new energy that you need for work and family. Of course, a hobby can be social, but by being alone once you have the freedom to do whatever you wish to your mind can rest for a moment, and you can go deep within and follow your inner voice. Lagom is about balance, and if you are usually very social, this is a way to find balance.

On the other hand, if you are less social, and prefer spending time alone, lagom might mean that you should put yourself out there more. This could look like creating time to spend with friends, family, and others. If you are generally quiet at work, try talking to your colleagues and ask them questions to spark conversation. Meet new people outside of work by joining a group or an association to share time with others who have like-minded interests. Meeting new people can bring fulfillment in life and joy to new life experiences.

Finding a balance between work and home life can be hard to accomplish, but it is completely possible. If you find yourself working hard with no time left for pleasure, then you might want to take a look at the situations You are able to control. The solution may not always be obvious, but by thinking about your options and asking friends, family or co-workers for help, a solution will arise. If you can, try talking to your boss about having too much on your plate, say no to colleagues who want help when you are too busy for your own work, or help each other out to succeed at the same goal. If you find that you are working at a dead-end job, try to find a new job or a new career. Everything is possible to achieve balance in your life.

Sorting out your priorities can be hard. To find the lagom balance, write a list of things you feel like you have to do and write a list of things you want to enjoy doing. Then, prioritize the list, putting them in order, starting with the most important. Throughout the day, cross them off as you go. The key here is doing a little of what has to be done and a little of what you enjoy doing. At the end of the day, both lists will have things crossed off so you can see what was accomplished. This will leave you feeling satisfied and content with how the day was spent. In other words, doing more with the time you have can help you enjoy moments of lagom with family and friends.

The Swedes are not better than anyone else at saying no, and prioritizing and enjoying their relationships and hobbies. Although they do have the concept of lagom to guide them, they don't think about how to spend more time with their families and friends. Perhaps the Swedish have a natural longing for solitude, helping them to stay balanced in their social engagements.

Lagom is a lifestyle to help you achieve balance within yourself and in your life. Spending time with family and friends while still enjoying hobbies and interests alone is important to your health and mind. Instead of striving for perfection, just do what you do as well as you can. No one will thank you for overdoing it instead of settling for a little bit less.

The next important matter when it comes to living a lagom life is how to create a good balance. The right amount of balance is up to you to decide. If you love your job and don't have anyone waiting at home, then feel free to spend more time at work. If you recharge by being surrounded by people, then spend more time with others. An introvert may need more time alone to feel balanced. Think about your wants, needs and obligations, and see what can be rearranged to achieve that balance in life the lagom way. Remember, everything in moderation.

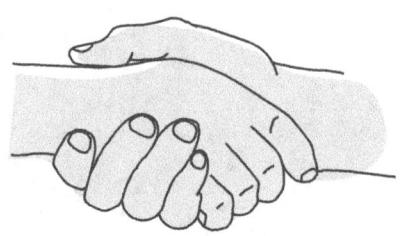

CHAPTER 5:
LAGOM AT HOME

CHAPTER 5: LAGOM AT HOME

Lagom is not only useful for creating harmony and balance between work and life or between socializing and time alone; it is also a useful tool to make your home a peaceful, relaxing and comfortable space to dwell in. In this chapter, you will learn to focus on creating the most peaceful home you have ever had - the lagom way.

Starting with the home itself and its decorations, there are a plethora of things to make your living space a cozy and comfortable place to be. Do you have any furniture not being utilized? Start with that. Get rid of furniture that is never used, to eliminate the clutter and fill your home with items that bring you joy and happiness. Then continue on, eliminating decorations, cushions, and curtains you don't like don't use in your home.

It's important, when working on your lagom lifestyle; to understand how to decorate your home in a way that is best suited to this concept. Remember that lagom is all about living a life that is not too little and not too much. This means that you shouldn't rush out and buy all new furniture to replace every item you own, especially when some of your existing furnishings may work just fine for a lagom home. On the other hand, it does mean you might want to cut back a little and make some different design decisions that can help you bring balance to your living space.

BEDROOM

- Try painting the walls white, off-white, or gray in your bedroom to create a cool and relaxed space. If you desire color, you could paint one of the walls and/or use colorful bedding.

- Decluttering is usually the first step toward creating a lagom bedroom of any kind. Clutter is common in bedrooms, so take your time organizing and don't forget to donate or sell any items you no longer wear that may be cluttering up your closet space.

- If you have a window in your bedroom, choose a window treatment that will allow you to let in light during the day.

- Don't hang too much on the walls, and take care not to set out a lot of knick-knacks around your bedroom either.

- For your bed sheets and covers, choose simple, soft, neutral colors and stick to solids instead of patterns or prints. Don't cover the bed with unnecessary decorative pillows, and consider removing the headboard and footboard for an even more minimal look.

Living Room

- Stick to beige or gray walls in your living room for the perfect lagom mood.

- Set out houseplants for a touch of nature and greenery to freshen up your living room. Remember not to overdo it with plants, however, or the space may look too cluttered.

- Go with sheer curtains at the windows to encourage more natural lighting.

- Use smaller area rugs instead of larger carpets to break up the space visually and help things look more minimal overall.

Kitchen and Dining Room

- The wall color in your kitchen should be cool and relaxing.

- Choose a wooden dining room table if possible to bring something natural into the space.

- Don't clutter your counter space. Put away appliances you aren't using regularly, and be sure to let everything have its own visual space to sit on the counter.

- Try choosing vintage chairs and other similar repurposed furniture in your kitchen and dining room.

CHAPTER 5: LAGOM AT HOME

BATHROOM

- White bathrooms are a great place to get started with lagom. Since many bathrooms are already painted white or off-white, you often won't have to worry about changing the wall color to get started.

- Try lighting candles in the bathroom, especially if you don't have the option to use a lot of natural light in this space. Be careful, however, not to leave these candles unattended and to only use them when you're in the bathroom.

- If clutter is a problem in your bathroom or if you have a very small bathroom, consider bringing in a set of simple white shelves with cloth baskets to store your must-haves and linens for easy access.

This will help clean up the space visually without making it too difficult to find what you need in your bathroom when the time comes.
Home is a place to relax, spend time with your family and escape from your social engagements, work, and demands from people outside. Having a home that includes things you love can bring joy, confidence, and happiness to you and others around you. Having a cluttered home can be overwhelming, which can bring stress to your life instead of relaxation. Remember that you own your things, not the other way around.

ELEMENTS OF LAGOM

- Lagom is about reaching a calm and peaceful state through decluttering and organizing your home.

- Lagom can be a great stepping stone to Zen, but the two can also exist separately.

- Lagom can be used to help you reach and maintain a happy and satisfying life.

ELEMENTS OF ZEN

- Zen is an Eastern philosophy that originated in Buddhism but has come to mean, in the Western world, a calm and meditative state of being.

- Zen can be achieved through lagom; decluttering can help you become more Zen.

- You can feel more energized and less stressed by reaching Zen through lagom.

- Connecting these two can let them work together to give you a wider perspective in the world.

When it comes to material goods, it is not better to have more. In fact, owning many things only gives you more to clean, more to replace when broken or worn out, and you will probably spend more time searching for lost items . You should absolutely have what you need, but don't fill your home with nice things only to fill empty space or to show off to occasional visitors. Instead, try to adopt a "less is more" approach to your home. How much your home should contain is up to you, as it is a matter of need and taste. Feel free to have curtains, cushions, a wine glass collection and those nice,expensive dinner plates you only use for Christmas, but take a look at your life and what you really need, what you think you need, and how much of everything you need. Don't forget to only keep and buy things you truly love and care for. Even if you need

CHAPTER 5: LAGOM AT HOME

an item, don't keep it if it does not make you smile. Sell the old one or give it away and invest in a piece that makes you smile instead. Remember, the definition of lagom is up to you and differs from person to person.

Many people say they need more storage space or smart solutions to store things in the already existing storage areas of their homes. What most people actually need is to clean out their spaces and sort out what to keep and what to get rid of. A home that is clutter-free is more harmonious, allowing you to come home from work feeling relaxed and comfortable. Of course, decluttering your home takes work, and it can take a long time before you are completely done, but once your home is properly organized and neat, you will find yourself at peace. There is always something to declutter, like that junk drawer in the kitchen or bedroom, or underneath the sink. Who knows, the process could become a hobby you enjoy!

Another cluttered mess that can impact the home environment and your life is your wardrobe. Getting dressed in the morning can be both a pleasure and torture. Many of us mere looking at our clothes and thinking that we have nothing to wear. Decluttering your wardrobe the lagom way can get rid of this anxiety-driven nightmare.

Begin by emptying your closet; is recommended to get a good picture of the state your current wardrobe is in. One of the best methods for decluttering your closet has been popularized by Marie Kondo, and it's a good idea to check out her suggestions and ideas if you're looking for more in-depth information. To summarize, pick up one item at the time and consider how much you like this item, how much you can identify with it and how useful it is in your everyday life. Only keep the things you use, love, and feel are right for you. It is not necessary to make it into a complete capsule wardrobe with a limited amount of pieces. The point is to keep it organized and simple so that you have a wardrobe that expresses your personality. Create a wardrobe where you can easily find the perfect combination for each occasion, where the clothes fit together nicely, and where clothes are made in materials of good quality.

After you have organized your current wardrobe and gotten rid of things you don't want, write a list of things you need to complement the rest of your wardrobe. Another great tip regarding clothes is to plan out your outfits for the week ahead, saving you time and agony in the morning. The Swedish use lagom to simplify their wardrobe and as a result, have more time for other tasks, such as making and eating a nice breakfast, instead.

We have talked about our homes and wardrobes, but how can you shop the lagom way? The Swedish love to shop, but they are conscious buyers. Being a conscious buyer means buying only what you need, considering quality over quantity and always following your taste. The perfect way to buy only what you need is by making a list. It does not matter if you are buying decorations for your home, clothes, or food; think about what you need and write a list. The Swedish love lists! Also, avoid impulse buying. If faced with a situation where you are standing in a store wanting to buy something, consider its use in your life. If you cannot come up with one, walk away. Also, think about quality over quantity so items can last longer when it comes to clothes, furniture, and decorations. This way, you buy fewer the things you will enjoy them for a longer time.

CHAPTER 5: LAGOM AT HOME

When shopping with moderation, think twice before buying anything. It may seem dull to shop the lagom way, but it can be delightful spending time looking for one perfect, thoughtful item instead of multiple not-so-good items. This will save you time and money, and you will become happier with each buy. Before shopping, consider the following questions:

- Do I need this item?

- When will I use it? (Think of at least one specific moment in the near future when you will wear or use this item.)

- Can I afford this? (Don't consider the price tag, instead consider how many times you can wear or use this piece. An expensive thing can cost less than a budget alternative if used more frequently than the cheaper option.)

- Do I want this for myself, or is it something I want because everyone else has it? (Only buy things you want; don't buy anything because someone else says so.)

- Do I already have this or something similar at home to use instead?

- Will I be able to sell this when I no longer find it useful (Even if you are uncertain about a purchase, determine if it can be resold later on. Selling things for someone else to use saves money and incorporates sustainable living habits.)

Sometimes an impulse can meet the criterias of a good bargain. If faced with an impulse buy, after using the questions above, use this trick: take a picture of it. Go home and sleep on it. If you are still thinking about the item and can envision its functionality in your home or life, then you can buy it. Most of the time we don't crave these impulses the next day, but if we do, it may be a good item to buy.

Buying the lagom way can bring happiness, joy, and comfort to you and others around you. Less things means more space and time. More space means that your home will be easier to clean and to keep things tidy on a daily basis. Now you will have more time for other hobbies or interests because you're not spending as much time cleaning. A wardrobe that is simple and easier to choose from will leave more time and energy for the day. Fewer things means more money. Selling the things you don't want to keep and earning extra money encourages sustainability. Decluttering your home will make it appear open, neat, and clean for guests and yourself.

All of these tips will save you energy and time to allow you to do things you love with the people you love. Declutter, stay organized and find suitable solutions to keep your living space tidy to turn your home into a relaxing and calm place where you find peace and recharge.

CHAPTER 6:
LAGOM HEALTH AND WELLBEING

CHAPTER 6: LAGOM HEALTH AND WELLBEING

Discussing the impact of lagom when applying it to relationships, life, and home can help decrease stress and increase time, money, and energy for things you want to enjoy. Lagom is not always about the materialistic relics in your home or how you feel in social outings; it can affect how you feel within yourself, too.

In Sweden, people like to move their bodies and exercise, not only because they need to achieve anything, but because of how it makes them feel. Swedish people might not be known for being the most competitive people when it comes to sports, but they do move frequently. They exercise every day, including taking walks and riding bikes instead of driving. They take the stairs instead of the elevator, and so on. The Swedish like to keep their bodies healthy, and in a recent poll, only 9% of Swedish people stated that they never exercise at all[1]. Marathon training, Viking races, and Iron Man races have become a trend lately for even the average Swede. Although these races are rather extreme, they have become increasingly popular. Despite the Swedish fascination for exercise and the positive impact it has on the body and mind, they are cautious not to overdo anything. Instead of exercises specially for the perfect body, they work out in order to achieve the accomplishment itself and for the feel of it.

But not all Swedes specially are interested in these extreme workouts, and even those who are dedicated to them are careful not to overexert themselves. They are careful to have lagom and balance between working out their bodies and their minds. Exercising is something that needs to fit into the work and life balance, and this can be challenging. They work to maintain a balance between activity and rest as well as between work and life, and instead of having only the toughest workouts, they go for a hike in the forest for a day or do something else that balances exercise with family life while still bringing tranquility. You can definitely have a balance and still keep up with an exercise routine.

Hiking and spending quality time with your family can be considered relaxing while still being physical activity. It is relaxing because not only are you working your body, your brain is also getting a mental rest while enjoying a hygge moment with family in the forest or by the sea. This can also aid in recovery and boost energy levels.

---

https://www.thelocal.se/20140325/swedes-work-out-the-most-in-all-of-europe-exercise-health-sport-sweden-eurobarometer

In general, the Swedish love spending time in nature. It does not matter if they are going for a run, spending the day with their kids in the park, or spending sunny summer days by the sea;. Spending time outside can boost your body because it keeps you active the sun delivers much-needed vitamins to the skin. Most of the time we are indoors working, studying, or spending time alone or with others, and we forget how much our bodies need us to stay active.

Health and well-being are not the only benefits of physical exercise. It is also relaxing and exercises the mind. We spend our days with a lot of incoming information, and it is hard sometimes to tune out and let the mind rest for a moment. In Sweden, meditation, mindfulness, and yoga have become increasingly popular in order to balance a hectic lifestyle. Not everyone loves meditation, and certainly not all people love yoga,but many things the Swedish do, such as spending time in nature, saying no to certain events to be with family, and taking time to recover is considered mindfulness and gives life a nice touch of lagom.

Closely related to the subject of health and exercise is your diet, The Swedish try to prioritize eating solid, home-cooked meals made with clean and healthy ingredients as much as possible. They prefer spending

CHAPTER 6: LAGOM HEALTH AND WELLBEING

mealtimes at the kitchen table with their families, and to most people in Sweden, good food is important to the overall well-being. They do eat junk food moderately but shy away from microwaveable dinners or anything containing chemicals. They use real butter despite the calories instead of eating light products that contain additives that are generally not good for your health. It is easy to find and buy organic food, and they are dedicated to buying locally produced food to support small businesses. Food transportation from non-local distributors can take time, and as a result,the food is not fresh once it reaches the store. Transportation also contributes to pollution which also encourage the Swedish to buy locally. They love to eat good food, but in the true sense of lagom they do not only want it to taste good, they also want it to be healthy.

Finding healthy food that is not chemically treated, organic and locally produced is easy in Sweden. You can find these foods both in the local supermarkets and in local farmers markets. For those who are inexperienced or don't have time to grocery shop, using websites like Blue Apron and Hello Fresh, can be helpful, since you can order your groceries online and have them delivered straight to your home along with healthy recipes.s. The ingredients used by these companies may not always be sourced locally, but they do come from family-run farms and are sustainably grown. There is something to fit every food choices in your life: vegan food, vegetarian, easy-to-cook food, and grocery bags with organic food if you would prefer that. The Swedish people strive to live the lagom way regarding their health. While you might find these concepts new and time-consuming, the Swedes do it quite effortlessly by incorporating several of these concepts together. For example, they relax from work by spending time outside with their families, and while doing this, they get exercise, relaxation and family time all wrapped up in one. They cook a delicious and healthy meal and eat with their family, which combines a healthy lifestyle and spending quality time with family.

In Sweden, the National Food Agency (NFA) provides guidelines on how to eat to get all of the important nutrients the body needs,there's a discussion amongst the Swedish whether they should be trusted or not since some of their advice is contradictory to certain people's beliefs regarding what is to be considered healthy food. This is not a proven fact, but in Sweden, people following specific diets, for example, Paleo and LCHF, dislike that the NFA recommends the Swedish to eat plenty of pasta, bread, and other carbs. Whether you trust these guidelines or not, they are created to help people live healthy lives by recommending a balanced diet. The NFA guidelines state to fill at least a third of your plate (preferably half of it) with vegetables and/or fruits, but the Swedish love their traditional dishes , but are not afraid to mix things up with influences from different corners of the world.

CHAPTER 7:
Lagom in the Kitchen

CHAPTER 7: LAGOM IN THE KITCHEN

To encourage a healthy lagom lifestyle, here are some classical Swedish recipes to try at home. As an added bonus, we have included some non-Swedish recipes that are delicious and fit the lagom lifestyle. There are also tips on how to make your own snack food, since making things yourself is usually healthier. This way you will get a nice overall view of how lagom can be applied practically to all aspects of life.

Before we get started, it is necessary to point out these recipes have been slightly altered. We have added some veggies to classical Swedish recipes, because when these dishes first became popular, the Swedish population did not have access to many vegetables due to the cold and difficult climate. Today, fruits and vegetables are imported, and the use of greenhouses has made it so that that access to these ingredients is easier than ever before. The Swedes now eat more veggies, salads, and fruits along with their meats and starches.

BREAKFAST

Breakfast is considered the most important meal of the day, especially in Sweden. It is common to eat cereals or granola with milk or yogurt, sandwiches, and porridge. Although there has been an increasing trend in eating overnight oats or drinking a smoothie, the traditional breakfast dishes are still the most popular ones. Here we share a recipe for simple granola that you can add your favorite flavors to and modify to your taste. You also get easy-to-make oatmeal porridge that will give you enough energy to last all the way to lunch without a mid-morning blood sugar crash.

HOMEMADE GRANOLA WITH YOGURT

INGREDIENTS

- 2 cups raw oats
- ½ cup natural mixed nuts (or nuts of your choice), raw
- ¼ cup sunflower seeds
- ¼ cup flaxseed
- ¼ cup coconut flakes
- 1 tbsp honey or maple syrup

1 tbsp olive oil
Cinnamon and cardamom to taste
Ingredients:
2 cups raw oats
½ cup natural mixed nuts (or nuts of your choice), raw
¼ cup sunflower seeds ¼ cup flaxseed
¼ cup coconut flakes
1 tbsp honey or maple syrup
1 tbsp olive oil
Cinnamon and cardamom to taste

DIRECTIONS

1. Mix all the dry ingredients together in an ovenproof dish with olive oil.

2. Season with Cinnamon or cardamom to it and bake at 300 degrees Fahrenheit for 30-45 minutes. To ensure the granola toasts evenly, mix the granola every 10-15 minutes while baking. If you are allergic to nuts, you can add some other grains and seeds. If you don't like cinnamon or cardamom, you can use other spices of your choice. Leave to cool down before putting it in a jar. Add dried fruits such as raisins, apricots or cranberries once the granol for a fruity flavor and added nutrition.

OATMEAL PORRIDGE

INGREDIENTS

1 part oatmeal
2 parts water
A pinch of salt

DIRECTIONS

This one is so easy it is fail-proof, and anyone can do it.

1. Take one part oatmeal and two parts water, add a pinch of salt and cook until the porridge is firm but not glue-like. If it is too loose, then

cook Longer; if it is too hard or has the same texture as glue, add more water and stir.

2. Serve the porridge with fresh fruits and berries and milk, if you like. Use almond milk, coconut milk, or lactose-free milk for a dairy-free alternative.

SANDWICHES

If you're a breakfast sandwich eater, there are some healthier lagom alternatives. In fact, the sandwich is not a bad option since it is versatile and you can make anything with a sandwich! Start with sourdough bread and fill it with a wide range of healthier options like hummus or cream cheese instead of butter, and top the spread with your favorite vegetables. Or, use a cream cheese spread and add cold chicken, some green leaves such as spinach leaves, arugula, or tomato with a yogurt dressing for the perfect flavor and texture. The options are endless!

If you prefer having eggs in the morning, eat up. Eggs are an excellent source of protein and good fats. Plus, the Swedish eat a ton of eggs, boiled, fried, or poached, on a sandwich. They also eat scrambled eggs and bacon for breakfast at times. Keep lagom in mind and eat everything in moderations; there really are no other rules here.

SWEDISH BREAKFAST SANDWICH

INGREDIENTS

    2 slices of rye bread
    ½ sliced radish
    Anchovies to taste
    1 egg

DIRECTIONS

1. Bring a small pot of water to a boil, then add egg while the water is boiling.

1. Bring a small pot of water to a boil, then add egg while the water is boiling.

2. Boil the egg for 6 minutes or to desired doneness.

3. Let the egg cool. Peel and slice the egg.

4. Toast or broil the rye bread and top with egg, anchovies, and radish.

CHAPTER 7: LAGOM IN THE KITCHEN

LUNCH AND DINNER

All of these recipes can be served as either lunch or dinner. Of course, the Swedish do eat out, but not on a regular basis. In Sweden, eating out is saved for celebrations and for an occasional indulgence, rather than as part of everyday life.

CLASSIC SWEDISH MEATBALLS

INGREDIENTS

- 2 tbsp olive oil
- 2 pounds ground beef, pork, or lamb
- 1 diced onion
- ½ cup breadcrumbs
- ¼ tsp nutmeg
- ¼ tsp allspice
- 2 eggs, separated
- Salt and pepper to taste

DIRECTIONS

1. Heat 1 tbsp olive oil over medium heat until just simmering, then add onion and cook 3 minutes, stirring occasionally. Remove onion from the skillet.

2. Combine ground meat with breadcrumbs, egg yolks, and seasonings. Mix until thoroughly combined but be careful not to over-mix.

3. Roll into about 24 meatballs.

4. Heat remaining olive oil and brown meatballs on all sides.

Serve the meatballs with boiled or mashed potatoes and brown sauce.

Traditional meatballs are served with pickled cucumbers and lingonberry jam with grilled tomato, a mixed salad on the side, green beans, peas or broccoli.

CHAPTER 7: LAGOM IN THE KITCHEN

STEAK WITH OVEN ROASTED POTATOES AND BÉARNAISE SAUCE

Here is another classic dish in Sweden that if for summer barbecue.

INGREDIENTS

- A steak of your choice
- Béarnaise (Homemade or store bought)
- 1 pound small red potatoes
- 1 tbsp olive oil
- Salt to taste
- Pepper to taste
- French herbs to taste

DIRECTIONS

1. Cut the potatoes in two or four, and season with olive oil, salt, pepper, and French herbs. Roast in the oven, 225 °C for about 30 minutes.

2. Season the steak with salt and pepper. Grill or fry steak to your preferred temperature.

Serve the steak with the béarnaise sauce and roasted potatoes. Serve with in-season vegetables along with grilled (or fried) tomatoes, asparagus or green beans. Add a mixed salad on the side, grilled (or fried) corn-cob or anything else you and your family like.

HOMEMADE BÉARNAISE SAUCE

INGREDIENTS

2 egg yolks
1 cup plus 1 tbsp butter
3 tbsp minced shallot
2 tbsp red wine vinegar
1 tbsp lemon juice
1 tbsp chopped tarragon
Salt and pepper to taste
Parsley to taste

DIRECTIONS

1. Melt 1 tbsp butter over medium heat, then add shallots and a pinch of salt to the butter and stir.

2. Add vinegar and turn to medium-low. Cook 4 minutes or until vinegar has mostly evaporated.

3. Turn to low and cook 5 minutes more, then remove shallots from skillet.

4. Melt remaining butter.

5. In a blender, combine lemon juice and egg yolks with 1 tbsp water and mix until smooth.

6. Turn the blender to its lowest setting and remove the lid, then slowly drizzle in the melted butter until it has been blended into the mixture.

7. Transfer to a bowl and stir in shallots and tarragon. Season with salt and pepper to taste.

CHAPTER 7: LAGOM IN THE KITCHEN

PASTA CARBONARA

While pasta dishes are primarily Italian, Swedish people have adopted them into their meals. One such dish is pasta carbonara. This is not the original Italian recipe, but a Swedish adaptation that can be altered to your tastes. Feel free to add more garlic, remove the parsley, use the entire egg instead of just the yolk and so on. Nothing can be done wrong in this recipe, as long as you enjoy the result!

INGREDIENTS

- 1 box spaghetti noodles
- ½ pound bacon
- ¼ cup heavy whipping cream
- 4 eggs at room temperature
- 1 cup Parmesan cheese, grated
- ¼ cup softened butter
- ¼ cup chopped fresh parsley
- Salt and pepper to taste

DIRECTIONS

1. Boil spaghetti according to packaging directions.

2. Cook bacon until very crisp, then let drain.

3. Beat eggs and cream together in a bowl until combined, then add Parmesan cheese, stirring gently to incorporate.

4. Add pasta to a pan or pot and toss with butter until the butter melts and coats the noodles.

5. Stir in bacon, sauce, and parsley, and mix to combine.

Serve pasta on top of spinach leaves and add a side dish of chopped tomatoes with olive oil and salt.

PANED HALIBUT FILLET WITH MASHED POTATOES

Of course, we cannot exclude fish from the menu since Swedish people eat plenty of seafood. The key to all fish is to keep it simple, like this plaice fillet . It is easy, tasty and most certainly a fail-proof dish to serve. If you can, try to get some fresh fish instead of frozen for the best flavor

INGREDIENTS

>1 pound Halibut fillet (fresh or frozen)
>1 cup breadcrumbs
>1 large egg
>1 pound potatoes
>Milk to taste
>Butter to taste

DIRECTIONS

1. Beat the eggs in a bowl until blended together. Set aside. Coat the plaice fillet in the egg mixture and bread it in the breadcrumbs; cover completely.

2. Fry the filet in butter in a hot skillet, about 3-5 minutes on each side. Boil the potatoes and mash them, adding milk and butter to taste. Serve the fish and mashed potatoes with a slice of lemon and a mixed salad of your choice. We recommend green peas, Brussels sprouts, broccoli, or a delicious ratatouille.

TOAST SKAGEN

This toast is more of an entree dish, and it is so delicious we could not possibly leave it out. Skagen is a place located on the Swedish west coast, but it is unclear why this particular dish was named after it. It is possibly connected with the west coast in Sweden, which is most famous for its seafood. However, this toast is a delicacy served not only in the west coast but in restaurants all over Sweden.

CHAPTER 7: LAGOM IN THE KITCHEN

INGREDIENTS

1 cup cooked and cooled peeled fresh shrimp
2 tsp lemon juice
2 tbsp mayonnaise
2 slices sourdough bread
3 tbsp sour cream (or creme fraiche, if available)
2 lemon wedges
1 slice butter
Dill, horseradish, and black pepper to taste

DIRECTIONS

1. Mix the shrimp with dill, horseradish, mayonnaise and sour cream, all according to your liking.

2. Season with salt, pepper, and lemon to taste.

3. Fry the bread in the butter until it is golden brown. If the bread is soaking up the butter, add more to avoid burning the bread.

4. Put the shrimp mixture on the bread. Garnish the toast with a dill, black pepper, and a lemon wedge.

These are just a few classical Swedish dishes that will make you feel satisfied without being too filling. They are delicious and easy to make with the capability to add more vegetables for added health benefits. When trying out these recipes, it is easy to understand why the Swedish have extra time to do all the things they want and need to do to achieve lagom in their lives. These recipes are simple to prepare and cook, leaving more time for enjoying free time and family.

JUNK FOOD

Junk food cannot be completely erased out of anyone's diet, even the Swedish, and we cannot write about lagom and food without mentioning junk food. Here are some tips that the Swedish use to enjoy junk food in a lagom way while still maintaining a healthy diet and lifestyle.

First and foremost, try to keep a balance. If you eat healthy and well-balanced most of the time, there is no reason why you should not enjoy junk food every once in a while. By all means, indulge yourself with a burger, some fries and a milkshake. Use the Swedish model of dining out and do it to spoil yourself instead of using fast food as a go-to everyday solution. We know that many fast food restaurants have begun serving healthier options, like carrot sticks instead of fries. But even in Sweden, fries and burgers simply cannot be separated. The healthy and conscious Swedish have figured out that if they eat healthy all the other days, they can enjoy junk food every now and then. Just don't indulge on a daily basis!

Furthermore, burgers and pizza can be made at home and are easy to prepare. Even French fries can be healthy if made at home, as the salt is controlled more than at a fast-food place. Make sure to use clean ingredients without additives or chemicals, and try to make the majority of the sauces and dough (for pizza) yourself. A homemade burger with pineapple, pickled onions, lettuce, and tomato, is not so bad. Besides, making it yourself will make you feel fuller faster and control how much you intake. Making your own fries by cutting potatoes and baking them with olive oil and salt in the oven instead of buying fries is a tastier and healthier alternative.

CHAPTER 7: LAGOM IN THE KITCHEN

Making your own pizza is also a healthier option, allowing you to choose fresh ingredients and control what goes in and on your pizza. Plus, it is a fun activity for the whole family to enjoy together.

It can be overwhelming cooking at home on most nights, but it is well worth the effort. In Sweden, gathering a few friends or family and cooking together is a great way to socialize.

If you prefer having eggs in the morning, eat up. Eggs are an excellent source of protein and good fats. Plus, the Swedish eat a ton of eggs, boiled, fried, or poached, on a sandwich. They also eat scrambled eggs and bacon for breakfast at times. Keep lagom in mind and eat everything in moderations; there really are no other rules here.

PIZZA DOUGH

INGREDIENTS

2-½ cup flour
1 tsp sugar
1 tsp salt
1 tbsp quick-rising yeast
1 tbsp oil
1 cup water

DIRECTIONS

1. Combine flour, salt, sugar, and yeast in a large bowl.

2. Combine water and oil, then add to the yeast mixture.

3. Flour a cutting board or another surface, then turn the dough mixture out onto this surface.

4. Knead for two minutes.

DIRECTIONS

5. Grease a bowl and place mixture into greased bowl. Cover and let stand for 20 minutes to rise.

6. Punch down dough and place onto a lined pizza pan or baking sheet. Shape into a circle or rectangle depending on the pan.

7. Bake at 400 degrees Fahrenheit for about 10 minutes.

8. Remove and top with any toppings, then bake for about 10 more minutes to complete the pizza.

9. Optionally, before baking, you can freeze or refrigerate the dough until you're ready to use it.

SNACKS

In Sweden, it is recommended to eat three larger meals and two snacks each day. This helps regulate blood sugar levels to maintain energy all day, eliminating the two o'clock crash and cravings. So, what is the Swedish snack of choice? It depends who you are asking and how old they are.

The younger children have something called a "fruit break" at school in the morning. Each child will have brought their fruit of choice in their school bag and they eat fruit together as a class. Even at home, most children are served a fruit when they crave a little something between meals. Sometimes the children are served plain yogurt along with the fruit to keep the hunger at bay a while longer if needed.

For adults, two snacks are not necessary, and most will not eat that much. The adults who do eat two snacks in-between meals will eat a fruit or plain yogurt with fruit like the children. Other common snacks are a boiled egg served with ham or another source of protein and/or a healthy sandwich. A smaller portion of the breakfast eaten as a snack or a smoothie are popular options too. The best of all is that these are all healthy and good options instead of consuming chocolate, a cookie or other sugary options. If you find yourself craving chocolate, try reaching for dark chocolate that is no lower than 70%. This is something that the Swedish indulge in every so often, but not every day. When adopting a lagom lifestyle, even when it comes to eating, the process is about finding a good balance. These changes will help you make better choices all day and in many ways. Snacking should be easy and convenient to carry and eat wherever.

When it comes to snack time, coffee is a popular choice for most Swedes. However, for those living the lagom lifestyle, it is important to not overindulge and make it a priority to find a balance. Picking the right meals for your lagom diet plan is a process that is all about balance. However, it's also important to choose foods that help you feel your best and encourage wellness at the same time. This may mean you're not eating quite as much as you're used to, or it might mean you have to rethink the types of food you reach for when you get hungry. However, making sure you choose good, quality foods and stick to the lagom principles with every bite you take can make a big difference in both your body and mind.

Picking the right food is only one aspect of eating lagom. Another important concept to keep in mind is that you should always remain balanced mentally while cooking and preparing your meals. Don't cook when you know you don't have time to complete the task, and don't overdo it by trying to prepare a recipe that sounds much too difficult for your skill level. A small challenge is always a good thing, but frustrating yourself will throw you out of the lagom mindset right away and may end up bringing some negative energies into your meal at the same time. While cooking, make sure you gather all the ingredients and tools you'll need before you get started. If you're following a recipe, keep it close at hand and take the time to double-check it to ensure your measurements are correct. This is just another way you can bring some peace and balance into your kitchen experience and give yourself a better chance at creating something successful at the same time. You may also want to make your cooking space a comfortable one by putting on some soft music in the background or opening a window for some natural air and light while you work.

CHAPTER 7: LAGOM IN THE KITCHEN

When you eat, once again, give yourself time to really enjoy the process so you don't feel rushed. Chew slowly and thoughtfully, considering the flavors that are present in the food. Try each individual item on your plate separately and then try it all as one composed bite to see how the flavors and experiences change. Stop every now and then to take a drink of water so you remain hydrated, as well. You may be surprised to see just how your dining experience can change when you take time to enjoy your food!

Last but not least, plan your grocery shopping and your meals ahead of time for a better lagom experience. One of the many ways you can create balance in your life is to make sure you stay organized. Choose meals at least one week in advance and write a grocery list so you don't have to wander around the market in confusion And don't forget to always choose dishes that can be prepared with natural, healthy ingredients! Stay away from pre-packaged meals and other similar items that are not going to fit into your lagom eating.

Chapter 8:
Lagom as a Way of Saving the Planet

CHAPTER 8: LAGOM AS A WAY OF SAVING THE PLANET

We have covered how lagom is applied in most Swedish homes and how you can use it to change your life. The question still stands: How does the lagom lifestyle impact the world on a global level? The lagom way might help save our planet with each individual living more modest lives and, therefore, respecting nature and switching to a more green lifestyle. The lagom lifestyle suggests you are conscious of your environment and the impact your habits have on it. As you strive for doing everything in moderation, take into account how moderation can lower your impact on the planet and the environment, like decreasing pollution and damage to ecosystems from littering. In this chapter, we will discover what you can do to lead a more environmentally-friendly life.

The lagom lifestyle is closely connected to conscious habits and buying the things needed and used for functionality instead of impulse buying on a "want" basis. When we spend our money on things we were taught to believe we should want, we are being wasteful. We are told by various ads in papers, magazines, on billboards, and in TV commercials to want all sorts of different things for ourselves, our homes and our children. But, that couldn't be further from the truth.

Often, we don't consider the materials that are used in the things we buy. This includes items we buy just to sit in the closet or in a drawer that will eventually be thrown out, adding to the landfills and trash in the oceans.. By applying the lagom way in your life and focusing on building a sustainable lifestyle, you will become more aware of how money is being spent and why. Sweden is actually one of the most environmentally-friendly countries to live in, and there is much the rest of us can learn from that.

When buying something, consider not only the quality of the item but also what materials are used and how it's produced. Pick a material that will last a lifetime and is produced in an eco-conscious way. Look for different terms on labels such as "eco," "cruelty-free" or "fair trade." There are several different labels like this, and they could vary depending on what country you live in. Read different certificates in your country or state, learn what they mean, and try to buy things that are produced that way. This will make an impact on the environment as well as the people producing them. For example, buying eco coffee means that the work environments for those working in the fields are healthier, pay is within the state or country regulations, and so on. Stay conscious of what you buy and how it affects other people. We are all not perfect, including the Swedish, but practice the lagom way often and question why you are buying things, what materials are used, and whether or not the item is sustainable for long-term usage. For example, watch out for materials in clothes that contain microplastics that wash out into the ocean during washing, or switch your ordinary coffee to an ecological brand instead. The taste will be better, and you'll be having a positive impact on the planet.

Before buying anything new, determine if you could find the same item at a thrift store or estate sale. Vintage has always been a thing in Sweden and particularly now it is a trend on the rise, where young people buy clothes and furniture from second hand shops, spending time altering the clothes or items to personalize them.

If you do buy new clothes, try to buy brands of good quality that will last throughout time. This is particularly useful for the basics in your wardrobe such as shirts, pants, jeans and so on. The Swedish prioritize a classical wardrobe so they can invest in high-quality items, rather than buying multiple cheap items that will have to be replaced each season when they become out of date.

CHAPTER 8: LAGOM AS A WAY OF SAVING THE PLANET

In Sweden, many are moving to the countryside away from the hustle and bustle of the city. Although there are many new homes being built, many choose to buy older homes outside the cities and villages. Many spend their time and money restoring the homes instead of building new homes in these areas, being environmentally-conscious to how construction of new homes can affect the planet. Restoring homes can have a satisfying effect on your body and mind, and rejuvenates older homes that would have eventually been torn down.

Being environmentally-friendly and conscious, many Swedish have been growing their own plants, vegetables, and fruits in their backyards or balconies. Growing your own food is a huge trend that can save you money. Another added benefit to getting your hands dirty with Mother Nature, is that gardening can be good for the mind and soul, and can provide quality time with your family. Remember to be lagom and incorporate low maintenance plants like tomatoes, berry bushes, or flowers that require little attention and time. Growing your garden can help improve the quality of the air around you, outside and inside your home. There are many benefits to incorporating nature in your home and surroundings. While other people are stressed in the cities, making changes to incorporate nature in your life can help the planet while helping you find peace at the same time.

There are, however, many things you can do to live the lagom way and saving the planet that do not involve moving or changing your shopping habits. In Sweden, things like plastic reduction, recycling, and zero waste efforts are popular in the lagom lifestyle. As a way to minimize your impact on the planet, bring reusable bags to the supermarket, buy sustainable, quality clothes, and minimize your waste. Also, the Swedish people love to recycle almost everything such as plastic, paper, glass bottles, tin cans, and so on.

Maya Thoresen

CHAPTER 9:
LAGOM CLOTHING

CHAPTER 9: LAGOM CLOTHING

When you're working on your lagom lifestyle, there's no reason why you can't include your wardrobe in the process, too. Your clothes can showcase lagom just like every other part of your life, if you know how to make them work for you. However, picking clothes that are lagom can be a little tricky, so be sure to take your time when doing this. Don't go overboard, and really stop to consider your purchases before making them. Remember, not too little and not too much is the way to go when you're shopping for lagom clothing items! Here are a few more tips to keep in mind:

- Balance, balance, balance. Remember that keeping lagom is all about making sure you don't swing too far in one direction or the other. This means that you shouldn't go wild with tons of different vibrant colors and strange styles, but it also means you don't have to feel like you're wearing a boring, drab outfit every time you step out of the house, either. Look for something that bridges the gap between both of these concepts and helps you look good without drawing an unnecessary amount of attention to the clothing at the same time.

- Function over form. The clothes you choose for a lagom wardrobe should be functional—and comfortable! You shouldn't be worried about how you look to others, but should instead focus on how the clothing works for you and how it makes you feel.

Always choose something comfortable and easy to move around in. You don't have to wear something that restricts your movement or is made of fabric you can barely stand to touch. You don't even have to wear uncomfortable shoes just because they look good!

- Pick items that are made to last and won't cost a fortune. You don't have to pay hundreds of dollars for a high-quality pair of pants when you can find a comparable item for fifty dollars or less. On the other hand, buying a pair of pants that's only twenty dollars but will wear out in less than a year of use isn't very good balance, either. Look for something middle-of-the-road that's made of durable materials but isn't on the high end of the pricing scale.

- Saving money and keeping things minimalistic is the most important factor in choosing clothes for your lagom wardrobe.. Be frugal and don't worry about stocking up on name brand items when an off-brand will work just as well for the same situations.

- Sustainability is important. One of the key facets of lagom involves making sustainable, green, eco-friendly decisions to help improve balance on a global scale choose clothes that are made from sustainable materials or produced in factories that don't contribute as much to pollution as others do. It may be tough to find these brands, but they're out there, and supporting them can make a big difference .

- Upcycle or recycle your clothes when possible. Turn them into something new or use worn out clothes for cleaning rags. Donate clothes that are still in good condition to local thrift stores and shelters, or ask members of your family if they can use them instead. Don't just throw them away!

- Last but not least, don't neglect spring cleaning for your lagom wardrobe! Once a year, go through your clothes and consider each item. If you haven't worn the item within the last year—during the correct season when you might've done so—then it's time to get rid of it. Even if you love it and feel like you're sure to wear it again in the future, just take a deep breath and donate or throw it out. Chances are good that, if the item didn't come into your mind as an option during the past year, that is not going to change in the coming year either.

Clothing is one of the many areas people tend to gloss over when they're planning their lagom lives. While clothing is one of the central concepts in hygge, it may not be the first thing on your mind when you're thinking of practicing lagom. There are several tips you can keep in mind when learning how to lagom your wardrobe, however, so take your time working through these concepts to help you get a better idea of what to expect from this overhaul. Be ready to get rid of some items and understand that you may not be buying new ones to replace those items as you go through this list.

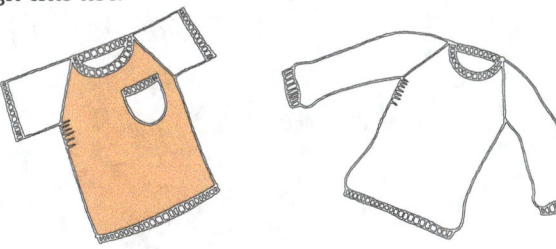

CHAPTER 10: LAGOM AND PARENTING

CHAPTER 10: LAGOM AND PARENTING

Did you know you can even apply the concept of lagom to your experience as a parent? Although parenting is a very personal matter and varies from family to family, many parents choose to incorporate lagom beliefs and elements into the way they raise their children. Perhaps not surprisingly, a lot of these ideas come from the way families in Sweden raise their children as well, and these concepts are becoming popularized throughout the rest of the world If you're interested in giving this a try, you should keep in mind the following suggestions:

- Let in some natural light—and natural air, too. Especially when your child is still a baby, consider opening the window to let in some light and air while your little one is napping. In Sweden, many doctors even recommend doing this to encourage the growth of a healthy immune system. Of course, if your baby has any health risks that could be aggravated by this, it's best to skip this suggestion and pick something else from the list of lagom parenting options. If not, however, don't be afraid to let your child breathe in some nature now and then!

- Spend as much time with your children as you can, but remember balance is key. Families in Sweden spend time together often and even take long, extended vacations together as well. Swedish parents play outdoors with their children and care about what's going on in their children's lives, too. On the other hand, it's important to keep things balanced and in check, and remember that your child is an individual. Children need their own private time away from parents and other family members sometimes, too, so respect your kids' boundaries while still making sure to spend time with them.

- Remember that it's okay to use childcare. In Sweden, parents tend to send their children to a childcare facility from an early age, and it's not frowned upon to do this when you need to get back to work after having a baby. Swedish daycares come in many variations and there are plenty of options out there for families to choose from. But keep in mind, too, that if you send your child to a daycare, you should set aside some time to spend one-on-one (or as a family unit) with your little one every single day to make sure all of their emotional needs are being met.

- For a true lagom lifestyle, children should be encouraged to play outdoors. Parents should also get involved and should either be active with their children while outside or should remain close by while children play. This is for safety as well as for the benefit of the whole family emotionally! Playing outside, getting active, and having plenty of access to fresh air and sunshine is an important part of the lagom life all year long. In Sweden, many families send their children out to play whether it's warm, cold, raining, or snowing.

Chapter 11: Lagom hobbies

CHAPTER 11: LAGOM HOBBIES

Are you interested in finding out how to keep lagom close to your heart even when enjoying your hobbies? While you're relaxing and enjoying the things that make you happy in life, you can remember lagom and work to achieve the balance you crave at the same time. You may even decide to take up some new hobbies that can be lagom, too, especially if you feel a little bit adrift without something to spend your free time on. Remember that lagom is about finding the right balance between work, time with family and friends, and time to yourself as well, and hobbies are an integral part of that!

- No matter what your hobby is, keep things in balance every time you enjoy it. You may be tempted to spend all your free time on your hobby, but remember that you should choose varied activities to create a true balanced lagom lifestyle. However, don't neglect to give yourself plenty of time to enjoy your hobbies as well. And if possible, consider bringing the people you love into your hobby, too, by showing them what you're working on or encouraging them to learn about it as well. When you share a hobby, you're enjoying even more lagom in your life.

- Don't let your work become your hobby. Many people—especially those who own their own business or work from home—have a tendency to let work and hobby time become one in the same. A hobby should be something you enjoy doing that does not cause you stress. If your hobby is bringing you stress, then it's time to take a step back and maybe look for something else to do while you emotionally process the source of the issue. It can sometimes be impossible to do this if your hobby is your job, however, so keep these two separate from one another.

- Don't underestimate the importance of some of the classic relaxation hobbies out there. You may be interested in something much different, but if you try one of these old familiar hobbies, you might find it's perfect for you after all. Try woodworking if you enjoy building things, take up painting or drawing if you feel like being creative, or opt for knitting, sewing, or crochet when you enjoy having a hobby you can bring along with you just about anywhere. These may seem like old-fashioned or "boring" choices, but they can make a big difference in a lagom life.

- Remember to remain frugal and don't overspend on your hobby. Yes, you might have a pricey hobby—such as classic cars, for example

—but you should still make sure to create a budget and stick to it when making purchases related to this part of your life. You probably don't need every hobby-related item you think about purchasing, and therefore it's a good idea to write these items down, wait a day or two, and then see how you feel about buying them. Chances are good you'll realize they're not all necessary, and you'll be able to spend your money only on those items required to enjoy your hobby instead.

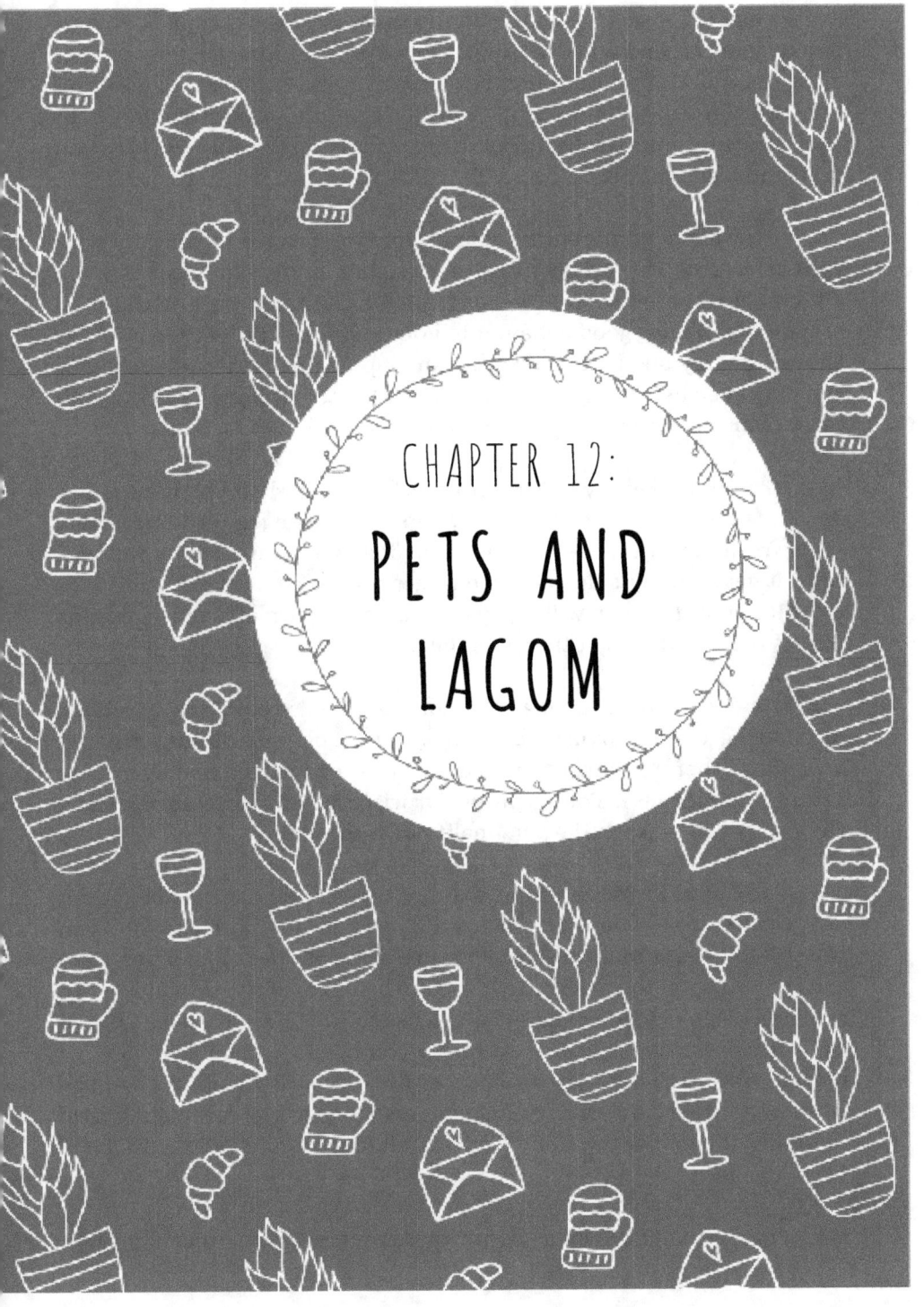

CHAPTER 12:
PETS AND LAGOM

CHAPTER 12: PETS AND LAGOM

Even when it comes to the furry (or feathery or scaly) members of your family, you can find ways to bring lagom into your life, too. Pets tend to bring joy more often than not, but they can also bring stress now and then too. Keep this in mind while you check out the suggestions below to help you determine the best way to incorporate lagom into the way you keep and treat your pets.

- Just like with parenting, you can create balance in your life with your pets, too. The proper way to discipline and train a pet may be difficult for everyone to agree on, but for the most part, it's best to practice rewarding good behavior in your furry friends. Getting into this habit from day one with your pets can help you balance their behavior and may even help bring a sense of calm to the whole household that will carry over into your pets' personalities, too.

- Get out and enjoy nature together! Particularly if you have a dog, don't neglect the time you can spend outside enjoying nature and getting some fresh air together. Walking your dog is a great activity for you, since it gets you outside and encourages you to be active. But it's also great for your dog, who will enjoy the chance to burn off some energy as well as bond with you at the same time.

- If your dog has been having behavioral problems—particularly related to chewing or destroying items that don't belong to him—most pet behavioral therapists will encourage you to try walking him every day before anything else. You might be surprised what a difference a short daily walk can make in the personality of your pup!

- If you have an indoor cat or another type of pet that cannot or does not go outdoors—even if you have a hamster or a tank full of fish—you can still find ways to bring a little nature into your pet's life. If you have a fish tank or a terrarium with a lizard, snake, or turtle living in it, research some pet-safe plants you can use in the tank to bring a little of the outdoors inside to your pet. And if you have a rodent that can't go outside and can't have real plants either, try just opening a nearby window a little bit every day for some fresh air. Just be careful not to do this when it could be too chilly for your pet or if it could allow a predator to get inside!

- Practice balance when choosing whether or not to bring home new pets, too. You may be an animal lover and might want to bring home every stray or needy animal you see. However, this habit is not lagom, and it's not going to bring you balance. Instead, it may cause you a lot of stress as your home becomes cluttered, destroyed, and overrun with pets. Take this into consideration as you carefully choose which pets are right for you and the other people in your household, too.

CHAPTER 13: SPORTS AND LAGOM

CHAPTER 13: SPORTS AND LAGOM

Sports are generally considered to be fast-paced, competitive, and filled with dynamic energies that certainly don't seem like they'd contribute very much to a sense of balance. However, you can still practice lagom in the way you approach sports and enjoy yourself in your favorite hobbies and activities at the same time. In this section, we'll help you learn how to manage your active sports lifestyle and encourage you to make the right decisions to keep lagom in your heart and mind at all times. You may find that your game even improves when you go into the competition with a refreshed, balanced mind.

- Remember that life is full of winning and losing, and that this in itself is a balance. You cannot win every game, because this means someone else would be losing every game in order for everything to balance out. Everyone has their time to enjoy the thrill of victory as well as the sadness of defeat, and a good sport should be happy for the other team even while feeling let down about losing. Understanding this concept can make it feel a little less disappointing when this ends up happening to you.

- Practicing your game is important, whether you play sports as a hobby or you make it a more professional or semi-professional part of your life. However, don't let practicing get in the way of other activities you need to attend to in your life. For example, don't neglect time with your friends and family because you have to practice constantly for the next big game. And don't take away time you may want to spend on other, more relaxing hobbies throughout your day-to-day life, either.

- Choosing to play a sport outdoors is already a lagom decision, since you'll be spending more time outside in the sunshine and fresh air when you play. However, if you play an indoor sport like basketball, you can still use this to your advantage and give yourself more of a chance to go outside when you practice, too. For example, although your official basketball games may be played inside, you can easily practice outside and can even get the whole family and all your friends involved in a game now and then, too.

- Don't forget to involve your kids in your sports lifestyle whenever possible! Kids may not be interested in more complicated adult sports like golf (although they might be more interested than you may expect), but they're likely to want to join in if you're playing soccer or softball in the backyard. These games may not be full sporting events, but they are a great way to teach your children healthy exercise habits, good sportsmanship, and the best way to remain lagom throughout every aspect of their lives, too. You can even use a family game to teach your children how to play a new sport, which can bring more balance to their lives as well. You never know when you might be teaching your child their new favorite hobby!

CHAPTER 14: LAGOM WHILE TRAVELLING

CHAPTER 13: LAGOM WHILE TRAVELLING

Taking a vacation from work can be an extremely relaxing experience. On the other hand, planning and executing a vacation—especially to a location you've never visited before—can be extremely stressful. Traveling may also be a strenuous time for you and your whole family, even though it's supposed to be a chance to have some fun and bond together. Practicing lagom throughout your travels and the whole time you're on vacation can help you stay focused, relaxed, and mindful of everything going on around you, and it can even help you form stronger, longer-lasting memories of the experience, too. Here are a few tips to help you get started.

- Make plans, but don't stress about sticking to them word-for-word. For example, you should definitely make plans when it comes to scheduling transportation such as taking a plane, bus, or train. You should also plan ahead of time and choose a hotel near the destinations you're planning to visit. From there, however, try to keep things loose and flexible so you don't feel bogged down trying to stick to a specific schedule every day. And don't be afraid to give yourself and your family some downtime to enjoy your hotel room or just lounge around by the pool, too.

- When traveling to another country, take the opportunity to bond with your family by learning some key words and phrases together in another language while you're there. You can also create memories and bonding experiences by trying new foods and visiting important landmarks.

- Always practice balance and be respectful when visiting cultures outside your own. You may not understand why a culture partakes in a certain practice, eats a certain food, or celebrates a certain holiday, but you can still be respectful and take the chance to learn a little more at the same time. You may be able to expand your worldview considerably when you do this, and in turn, you might find a new level of balance in your heart and mind, too.

- If you'll be traveling to a hectic destination, like a major theme park or a busy beach, encourage everyone in the family to take some quiet time in which they can nap, read a book, learn about the surrounding area, or listen quietly to a favorite album. Even if this quiet time only lasts an hour, it can provide a valuable reset in the middle of a busy and sometimes overwhelming day.

- Never be afraid to take a vacation that's really just for relaxing. You may feel like you need to plan lots of activities, especially if you have younger kids in your family or are traveling with a big group. However, you shouldn't underestimate how vital it can be to just get together and have fun with some different scenery for a little while. Consider renting a large cabin in the mountains together with your extended family and spending that time cooking outdoors, fishing, hiking, and enjoying nature. This is just one example of a true lagom vacation experience.

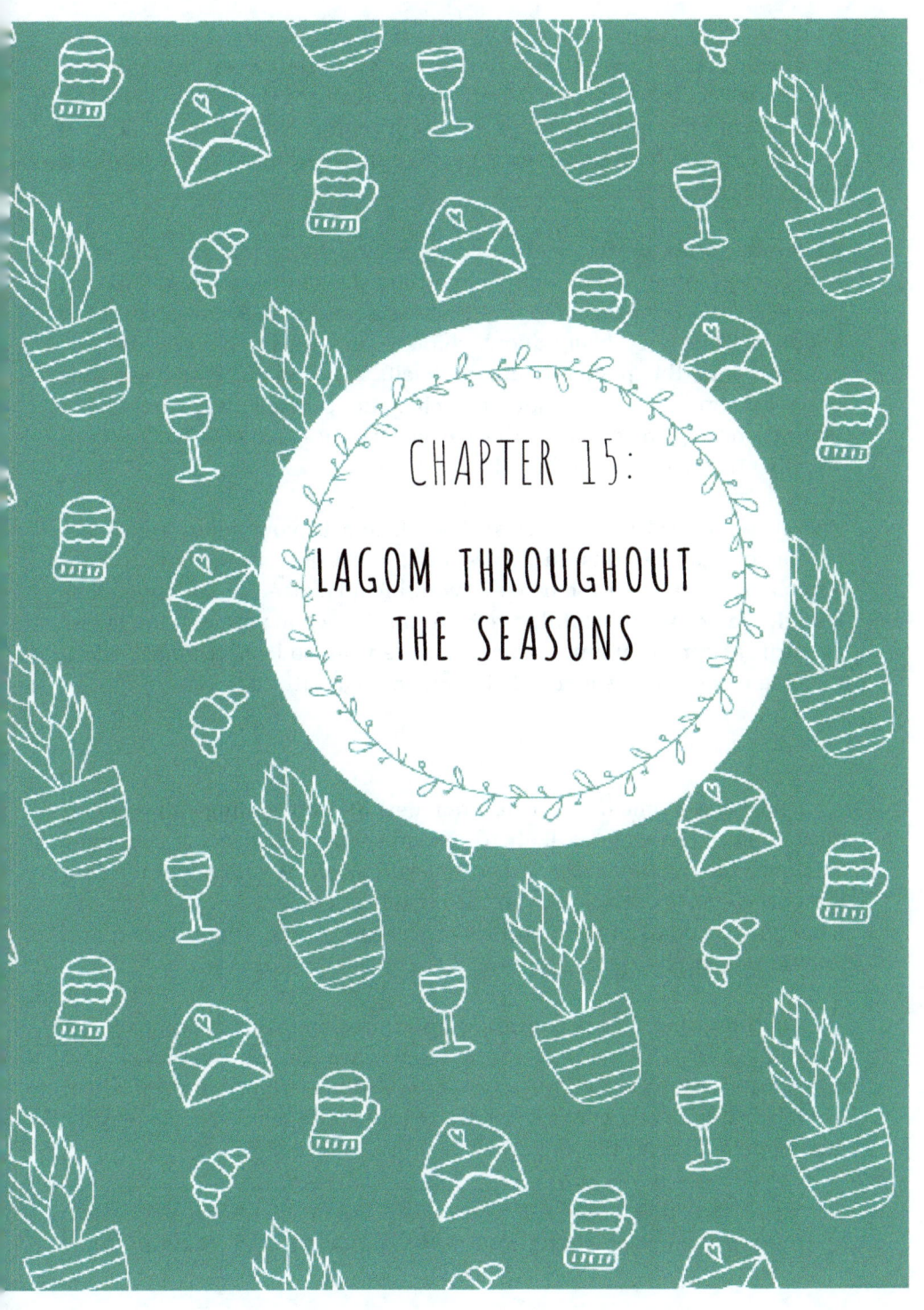

Chapter 15:

Lagom Throughout the Seasons

CHAPTER 15: LAGOM THROUGHOUT THE SEASONS

As the seasons change, the way you approach lagom will change as well. However, just because the year is progressing that doesn't mean you should neglect lagom at any point. The changing of the seasons and the celebration of various holidays can help remind you of what balance truly is and can help you keep a positive frame of mind when thinking about this balance, too.

Remember that tentir world and everyone living on the planet is balanced by time. We all experience time the same way, and this can provide a sense of peace and mindfulness to anyone who stops to think about it. Time may bring about changes, but those changes are just another way the planet balances itself. Even as different weather patterns approach throughout the changing seasons, this, too, is the planet working to maintain the perfect balance it needs to continue spinning through space in just the right way.

There are several ways you can keep lagom in your mind and heart throughout the seasons. In this section, you'll find suggestions to help you maintain balance and peace in your life no matter what time of year it might be. It can be helpful to refer to this list when you feel a little lost or adrift at certain points throughout the year, so keep it handy when you need a quick refresher to help you on your path to lagom.

SPRING

- Spring is a time of balance, when new life is blooming and growing outdoors and changes are likely to be made in many aspects of your own existence too. As the world wakes up again after the cold of winter, this is an excellent time to reflect on the meaning of balance in your life and what you can do to improve the sense of peace you experience when you practice lagom.

- In the spring, focus on cleaning and refreshing your living space for the coming year. This is a great time to go through your wardrobe and check it for any items you might not be wearing anymore. If they're still in good shape, donate them; if not, try to repurpose them in some way by adding them to a rag pile or gathering fabric for crafting.

- This is a great time clean the floors, windows, and other often-neglected parts of your home as well. Take time to really get into every corner when you do your spring cleaning and your home will be ready for the coming year in no time.

- Consider re-organizing your work space if you have an office job or something similar, too. There may be ways to make your job more efficient that you haven't even considered before, and you might be surprised at what a difference a little organization and change of scenery at the workplace can make, too.
- Take time during the spring to think of ways you can get involved with outdoor activities. Although it may not be quite warm enough yet to go outside often, depending on where you live, this is a good time to start branching out and encouraging kids to play outside longer in the evenings as the days lengthen, too.
- If you're thinking of getting a new pet, this can be a nice time of year to do so. Getting a pet in the spring gives your family time to get to know this new addition before summer rolls around and the kids will be home from school. However, don't get a pet if you're not financially, mentally, and physically prepared to take care of it, as this may throw off your balance and negatively impact the lagom in your household instead.

SUMMER

- In the summertime, plan to spend much more time outdoors, preferably engaging in physical activities with the whole family. This is the best time of year to play sports or to enjoy hiking, biking, swimming, and many other outdoor hobbies. Teach your children to exercise and get lots of fresh air during the summertime. And don't be afraid to spend some of that time relaxing and having a meal with your family, too!
- Since school is out during the summer, make plans to travel and take a vacation with your family. Remember the tips in the Travel chapter earlier in this book to help you make the most of your vacation experience while sticking to your lagom lifestyle. Keep in mind that over-stressing about your vacation isn't going to be relaxing for anyone involved, so you may be better off planning a small "staycation," especially if you don't have the money in your budget for something more extensive.
- Summer is a great time to try new recipes and learn something about cooking, too. This is the time of year when many families get together at least once, and sometimes a lot more often than that, to share meals and have fun with each other. If you're getting together with

- your extended family, why not take the opportunity to learn to make something new? You might even want to share that experience with family members you don't see often, like favorite cousins, aunts, or uncles.
- Let your hobbies shine during the summer, when you have more time to focus on fun. Whatever your hobby might be, this is a great time to learn something new about it. Strike a balance in your life by giving yourself time to work on your hobbies without overdoing it, and make sure you're still taking care of your family and work needs at the same time. You might even consider learning an entirely new hobby during the summer months!

FALL

- This cozy time of the year is the best time to start practicing your hygge, but there's no reason why you can't do a little lagom improvement during the fall, too. Try working on the way you balance your "me time" with your work and family time during the fall season. Set aside more opportunities for a little quiet time to yourself as the weather starts to get a little cooler.

- The nights will be getting longer at this time of the year, so why not consider a few more activities that you can enjoy after the sun goes down? You may want to sit outside and chat with your friends and family in the cooler night air during the fall, since insects won't be as prominent and the temperature may be more comfortable. This is a good time to reconnect with friends you might have lost touch with during the hectic summer months, too.

- Take time in the fall to pamper yourself. Give yourself one night a week, if you can, to take a long bubble bath and enjoy the time alone without the stressors of the rest of your life. Restore balance in your heart and mind by lighting some aromatherapy candles, putting on some soft music, and maybe having a small glass of wine or some caffeine-free tea to help you wind down after a busy work day.

- During the fall, you may plan big, hearty meals with your family and possibly with your friends as well. This can be an excellent way to bring balance to your family life, but make sure you set aside the time it takes to prepare these meals and enjoy them without pushing yourself beyond your limits emotionally.

WINTER

- Many family-oriented holidays occur during the winter months, so keep this in mind when working on your lagom lifestyle. This is a time of year when families get together a lot more often and share experiences with one another, but it can also be stressful for those who plan these gatherings. If you're going to be doing a lot of cooking or other planning for your extended family, don't forget to take time for yourself too. This is especially crucial during the holidays.

- Try decorating in a lagom way for the holiday season. It can be tempting to throw a lot of lots and sparkly garland around your home, but this isn't really a balanced way to decorate. Keep things simple, minimalistic, but effective. Stick to silver and gold or opt for white lights instead of rainbow-colored ones. Light candles to create mood and ambience, and play soft background music rather than letting loud holiday movies blast on the television all day long.

- If you have children, encourage them to understand that less can be more. During the holiday season, kids end up wanting a lot of new toys and other items thanks to the commercialization of many holidays. This can be a teaching moment for you and your family to learn a little about what it means to get something of value, and to help your children understand the concept of quality over quantity.

Once you figure out the best way to keep lagom going all year long, you'll be able to put these concepts into practice year after year. With more experience, you'll be better able to remember how you incorporated the practice into your life from the previous year and be more prepared to face whatever may come your way.

CHAPTER 16:
21-DAY LAGOM CHALLENGE

We will wrap this book up with twenty-one different challenges to give the Swedish lifestyle a chance and find out if it is a fit for you. Challenge yourself to adopt the lagom lifestyle and have an open mind. Be sure to track your progress in a journal during 21 days to see what works for you and your family. Some of the challenges will seem huge and need more time than just a day to adjust, but choose a small area of your life or home to change and narrow it down little by little. Once you feel confident with a change, continue on with another change until the lagom lifestyle is achieved.

Here's a list to help aid you on your way to achieving the lagom way:

1. KITCHEN AND DINING ROOM

Instead of attending or hosting a party, meet up with your closest friends and have some hygge time. This might include something simple as a good cup of coffee at a local coffee shop or having a simple dinner at home. The possibilities are endless.

2. SELF-CARE

Schedule some alone time today and do something that recharges your batteries. It could be a walk in the forest or a trail, a bubble bath, or staying in bed reading a book for a while in the morning or in the evening. The key is to find tranquility with yourself.

3. SPEND TIME IN NATURE

Get outside and enjoy what's around you. Take a walk, ride your bike, or do anything to get you moving. Spending time close to nature is good for your body and soul.

4. TRY SOMETHING NEW

Why not try a new hobby today? Do something you don't think you'll enjoy doing. You might be surprised. Or, do something that you are afraid of doing, like skydiving or going to a new town to explore. If you feel uncomfortable doing it yourself, bring a friend.

5. TAKE UP AN OLD HOBBY

Rekindle those old hobbies you use to enjoy. Sometimes we quit doing things without even knowing why when life gets too busy. This will help find peace and tranquility with yourself and your life.

6. SAY NO

Today's challenge is to say no to something. The Swedish are people pleasers, but they are willing to say no to things they don't have the time for or feel like doing. Say no to something today, and you'll be surprised at how calm you may feel afterward. Remember, you can't do everything every time for everyone.

7. SETTLE FOR GOOD ENOUGH

If you are a perfectionist, this will be hard. Sometime today, when you are performing a task, challenge yourself to leave your task once it is done. If you have done it properly, consider it done if it is good enough even if you don't find it perfect. Try it and see what happens. If you don't feel comfortable doing this at work, try at home. When cleaning, settle when it is clean even if there still might be some little thing left to clean. Don't overexert yourself to accomplish perfection each time. No one will probably notice the small imperfection anyway.

8. DECLUTTER YOUR HOME

Choose a room or small space to start the decluttering process. Do not take on your whole home as it will become overwhelming and discouraging. Tackle a drawer, a cupboard, or closet first, or even your desk, to declutter and open up space. Ask yourself questions to assess in the decluttering process:

- Do I use this item on a regular basis?
- Do I need this item (if yes, make sure you know what you need it for)?
- Do I love this item?
- Do I need more of this? (Ask this question if you already have multiple similar items.)

Only keep the things you use and need. Not all items are useful; some are only decorations and can stay as long as you like the item and as long as it has a given place.
Once you are done, organize what is left and get rid of the clutter through donation or reselling.

9. DECLUTTER AND ORGANIZE YOUR WARDROBE

Go through your closet and get rid of the things you no longer use or like. Instead of throwing them out, donate them or sell online. After you have decided what will stay, go ahead and organize your wardrobe, so it is easy to find everything. If this challenge seems too hard or becomes overwhelming, narrow it down. Choose one area to begin with, like cleaning out your underwear drawer and organizing it properly. Then continue on with the rest another day.

10. CHOOSE OUTFITS FOR A WEEK AHEAD

Organizing your clothes is one step. Today, plan out your outfits for the week ahead and stick to them. If this seems overwhelming, plan a few days ahead until it becomes a habit you enjoy doing. Planning outfits in advance can save time and energy in the morning. Your clothes are put together already, making getting dressed easy and efficient in the morning.

11. GO VINTAGE SHOPPING

Shopping at thrift stores and online second hand retailers helps recycle old clothes and adds personality to your wardrobe and home with unique and one-of-a-kind items. If you don't find the perfect use of your imagination and see if you can find something that is easy to alter and incorporate it in your home or wardrobe.

12. EXERCISE OUTSIDE

Leave the gym and take your exercise outside. Take in the fresh air and all the benefits of being outdoors. You don't need much equipment or special workout clothes. Lace up your running shoes, throw on comfortable clothes, and go for a brisk walk or run. Feel the need for some strength training? Stop and do pushups and sit-ups, or do them once you get home.

13. SWITCH SIDES

If you are usually active and social, try a mindful and calm exercise like yoga or meditation. If you are more of yoga and meditating kind of person, then try an intense and social activity like a spinning class or dance class. While mixing up your workouts will help maintain your body, it's a perfect way to find a balance between being social and being in solitude while finding the lagom way in your exercise routine.

14. PLAN OUT MEALS FOR ONE WEEK AHEAD

Write a meal plan for a week for breakfast, lunch, and dinner, and stick to that shopping list and menu. Make the plan according to your taste and circumstances and put it in writing so you will not forget it. If you want more of a challenge, choose dishes with similar ingredients so that you don't have to buy as many items at the grocery store. You can buy less and make sure to use all the food you buy, so you don't have to throw anything away.

15. WRITE A SHOPPING LIST AND STICK TO IT

Write a shopping list and stick to it at the grocery store. Don't forget to buy other essential items such as toilet paper, detergent and so on. This will help you save time, money, and the energy not to go back to the grocery store multiple times in the week. The more often you go shopping during the week, the more likely you are to impulse buy.

16. SWEDISH COOKING

Instead of going out for dinner, try cooking for yourself and eat at home. If you don't have a family who is eating with you, invite a few friends to keep you company. Try a Swedish dish included in this book. If you want to challenge yourself further, make extra food and bring the leftovers to work for lunch the next day and save some money.

17. PACK A SNACK

Try out a healthy snack instead of coffee and chocolate this afternoon. Prepare a nice and simple snack, like a fruit or a healthy sandwich, to eat when you feel those afternoon cravings kicking in.

18. DIY JUNK FOOD

Gather with your family or friends and cook your own junk food. Make pizza or maybe fries and burgers. The choice is yours. Find a recipe you like and just do it. Eat and enjoy.

19. RECYCLE YOUR GARBAGE

Gather your trash and recycle it. The Swedish do it all the time. Recycle everything from paper to plastic, and clothes. It is all according to the lagom way, and part of environmentally responsible lifestyle.

20. EDUCATE YOURSELF

The Swedish apply a lagom approach to their shopping habits and how they buy things because they read about products that are earth-friendly. So today, read up on environmental-friendly and/or cruelty-free labels. Consider switching over to these brands as they are more sustainable options, which is better for the planet.

21. SWITCH TO A FRIENDLIER OPTION

Try to use eco, fair trade or cruelty-free products instead of fast and cheaply made items. For example, if you are buying new facial products see if you can find an eco-friendly choice or buy ecological fruits the next time you visit the grocery store. Another thing you can do is try to find locally produced products to buy. When buying locally, you are supporting your community. Farmers and small business people will love you for it.

14. PLAN OUT MEALS FOR ONE WEEK AHEAD

Write a meal plan for a week for breakfast, lunch, and dinner, and stick to that shopping list and menu. Make the plan according to your taste and circumstances and put it in writing so you will not forget it. If you want more of a challenge, choose dishes with similar ingredients so that you don't have to buy as many items at the grocery store. You can buy less and make sure to use all the food you buy, so you don't have to throw anything away.

15. WRITE A SHOPPING LIST AND STICK TO IT

Write a shopping list and stick to it at the grocery store. Don't forget to buy other essential items such as toilet paper, detergent and so on. This will help you save time, money, and the energy not to go back to the grocery store multiple times in the week. The more often you go shopping during the week, the more likely you are to impulse buy.

16. SWEDISH COOKING

Instead of going out for dinner, try cooking for yourself and eat at home. If you don't have a family who is eating with you, invite a few friends to keep you company. Try a Swedish dish included in this book. If you want to challenge yourself further, make extra food and bring the leftovers to work for lunch the next day and save some money.

17. PACK A SNACK

Try out a healthy snack instead of coffee and chocolate this afternoon. Prepare a nice and simple snack, like a fruit or a healthy sandwich, to eat when you feel those afternoon cravings kicking in.

18. DIY JUNK FOOD

Gather with your family or friends and cook your own junk food. Make pizza or maybe fries and burgers. The choice is yours. Find a recipe you like and just do it. Eat and enjoy.

19. RECYCLE YOUR GARBAGE

Gather your trash and recycle it. The Swedish do it all the time. Recycle everything from paper to plastic, and clothes. It is all according to the lagom way, and part of environmentally responsible lifestyle.

CONCLUSION

Now that you've had a chance to read through this book, you should have some ideas of what to expect when you give lagom a try. You may be able to more clearly define the goals you want to set out for yourself, and you'll be prepared with suggestions to back you up every step of the way. You may have even learned more about lagom than you ever thought possible!

Take your time considering how you want to implement the concept of lagom into your daily life. From there, you can use the information in this book to guide you as you bring lagom into your home and your heart. Good luck, and remember: balance is key!

Thank you!

www.ingramcontent.com/pod-product-compliance
Lightning Source LLC
Chambersburg PA
CBHW050508240426
43673CB00004B/148